THE ULTIMATE GUIDE TO HYPNOSIS

WHAT YOU NEED TO KNOW TO GET THE CHANGE YOU WANT

JOHN O. WYLIE, CHT, MNLP

CONTENTS

INTRODUCTION:
MY STORY & THE PURPOSE OF THIS BOOK

Before I introduce this book let me introduce myself. My name is John Wylie and I am a hypnotist and hypnotherapist with over a decade of experience.

I had my first real exposure to the power of hypnosis in my mid 20s. I vividly remember how I felt as I listened to the story of my friend's mother, who for years struggled with debilitating cluster headaches. She told me about how terrible they were and how powerless she felt each time they overcame her. The best doctors she could find were of little help, drugs were inadequate and she feared the severe side effects. Nothing she tried worked. I recall how badly I felt for her as she told me how her terrible headaches ultimately drove her to the brink of suicide.

Fortunately, one of her doctors mentioned a colleague who was skilled in hypnosis. It was hypnosis that finally proved to be the answer she had been searching for. Finally, she was able to overcome the pain and reclaim her life. I was deeply moved by her experience and profoundly impressed by the power hypnosis had to end those headaches and give her a better life.

Years later, as I started a new job selling insurance, I remembered what I had learned about my friend's mother. My job was important to me and I wanted to be the best salesperson I could be. I wondered if hypnosis could help me reach my full potential. So, I began to learn more. The more I learned, the more excited I became. I did research and read over a dozen books but I wanted more.

I decided to go to a reputable hypnosis school in Washington state to learn from experts to do the exciting things I was reading about. It was expensive but I scrimped and saved and was finally able to go. That training changed my life. It inspired me to become a hypnotherapist so that I could help people unleash the power of their subconscious mind to overcome their problems and transform their lives for the better.

Since that first training, there have been many more trainings, courses, workshops, certifications, and years of practice. For over a decade I have continued to read, continued to study, and continued to learn directly from the best hypnotherapists. I have applied my learning to helping my clients get amazing results.

Over the years I have read literally hundreds of books on hypnosis and related subjects, most of them several times. I am pleased to say that I am more excited about hypnosis now than I was back then. And I'm so pleased that you are here learning about it for yourself. Like my friend's mom, and countless others, hypnosis can change your life as well.

Most people find hypnosis fascinating. Hypnosis is one of those subjects that easily captures people's attention, and rightly so. The fact that you are reading these words means that you are likely one of those curious and clever people who welcome the opportunity to learn about your mind and how you can use it's power to make your life better. Good for you! I think we'll get along famously.

While nearly everyone has heard of hypnosis and has a concept of what it is and what one might do with it, most people have gotten this concept from Hollywood or from seeing a stage hypnosis show. Unfortunately, the purpose of these sources is pure entertainment. It makes sense that they will not necessarily give you a true and accurate understanding of hypnosis.

Frankly, the vast majority of people don't really understand hypnosis very well and that is very unfortunate because, as a hypnotist and hypnotherapist, I have seen hypnosis do truly amazing things. And I'm not talking about making people do silly things on stage. Hypnosis is really **cool** for probably many more reasons than you think.

I have seen the power of hypnosis fix lifelong problems and transform people's lives for the better. The purpose of this book is to give you a solid understanding of hypnosis so that you can use it to make your life much better... more free, happier, healthier, wealthier. Whatever "better" means for **you**.

I acknowledge there are many, many books out there about hypnosis. I have probably read most of them. While they all contain valuable information, the majority of them are written for clinicians, academics or hypnosis professionals such as hypnotherapists, psychologists or even professional stage hypnotists. Most are written to teach you how to be a hypnotist. This is **not** one of those books.

This book is for the person who wants to understand the truth about hypnosis and how to use it to make your life much, much better. My goal is to give you the information you need and want, in easy to understand terms, so you can move past the myths and misconceptions and begin to learn the true power of hypnosis. You will soon learn that the power of hypnosis is really the power of your own mind. The best part is, it can help you fix your problems for good, overcome challenges big and small, and give you more of the good stuff you want in your life.

To keep things simple, I have divided this book into three parts. **Part One** will teach you the basics; things like how the mind works, what hypnosis is and what it is not. This section will answer most, if not all of those burning questions you would ask if you were to sit down and talk with me one-on-one.

In **Part Two**, we will focus on specific ways hypnosis can help people enjoy a better life. We'll talk in detail and in depth about things such as how to use hypnosis to lose weight and keep it off forever, how hypnosis can help you stop smoking, how to overcome fears and phobias with hypnosis, improve your golf game with hypnosis, use hypnosis to enjoy the best sex of your life, how hypnosis can help you bust stress and anxiety, and much, much more.

In **Part Three**, I will teach you a simple way to do self-hypnosis so you can hypnotize yourself whenever you choose. There are so many benefits to using self-hypnosis and I'm going to tell you, step by step, exactly how to do it. I'll even share an insider secret to make your self-hypnosis ten times more powerful. Cool stuff, right?!

In addition to all that, when I first learned about hypnosis I was skeptical. So, for the benefit of those who value a discussion of sound science and solid evidence, I have included an entire section on the scientific evidence proving the effectiveness of hypnosis for a wide variety of issues. You will find this information in **Appendix I**.

In **Appendix II**, I have compiled a partial list of well known leaders, scientists, musicians, actors, and other celebrities who have all used hypnosis to solve various problems, reach goals, or excel in their chosen field.

PART ONE:
THE BASICS OF HYPNOSIS

HOW THE HUMAN MIND WORKS

In this section I'm going to explain how the human mind works as it relates to hypnosis and, of course, from the perspective of hypnotherapy. Below you'll find a helpful chart that shows an overview of the concepts we'll be talking about here. We will be covering four major parts of the human mind: The Conscious Mind, The Critical Factor, The Subconscious Mind, and The Unconscious Mind.

Conscious Mind	Critical Factor	Subconscious Mind	Unconscious Mind
Point of Focus Analytical Logical Limited Capacity	Comparing Mechanism Resists Change	Starts out Empty Database of Information Holds Beliefs & Habits Generates Emotions Has Unlimited Capacity Motivates Toward Needs	The Body's Mind Autonomic Nervous System Source of Our Instincts Limited Ability to Change Generates Feelings
Protects against Perceived Dangers	Protects against Unnecessary Changes	Protects against Known Dangers	Protects against Infection & Controls Reflexes

I'm going to teach you about each one of these components of the mind. Each one has different functions and characteristics that are important to understanding how the human mind works. This information will give you a solid foundation to understand how hypnosis and hypnotherapy work.

I'm also going to explain how each part of the mind has a protective function. No matter how deeply you go into hypnosis you are always safe because all the components of the mind are always working to make sure you're safe.

THE UNCONSCIOUS MIND

Let's start with the unconscious mind. It's helpful to think of the unconscious mind as the mind of the body. Medical people will call it the autonomic nervous system. When we are born, we come into this life with instincts which are an inner awareness of how to operate our body. All animals benefit from instincts.

The unconscious mind is responsible for things like our breathing, heartbeat, blood flow, and many, many other processes and functions that go on automatically in your body, behind the scenes so to speak, without you needing to think about them.

One of the interesting things about the unconscious mind is that it's ability to learn is fairly limited. The unconscious mind can change and it can learn, but in our daily activities it isn't very good at it. Dr. Ivan Pavlov showed that the unconscious mind can learn through a process known as "classical conditioning". It was discovered that after ringing a bell and giving a dog some food a number of times, the dog would begin to salivate just from hearing the bell. This shows us that the unconscious mind can learn, because salivation is not under the control of the conscious mind. It's controlled by the unconscious mind or what is known as the autonomic nervous system.

So, the unconscious mind can learn through classical conditioning. It can also learn through hypnosis or hypnotherapy. For example, take someone who suffers from phantom limb pain. People who experience phantom limb pain have undergone an amputation but continue to feel pain where there is no longer any limb. This pain is clearly caused at the unconscious level for a number of different reasons. Through hypnosis we can re-educate the unconscious mind and eliminate that pain.

Now, another job of the unconscious mind is to generate how emotions feel in your body. For example, if you're happy (an emotion), then there are certain physical sensations that go with that emotion. If you feel angry or sad, your body is going to feel a certain way that is associated with those emotions. The unconscious mind generates the physical attributes of our emotions and we call those emotionally driven sensations in our body "feelings".

One of the important things I mentioned earlier was the fact that even at the deepest level of your mind, at the unconscious level, you have a protective function. No matter what you're doing or thinking, whether you are paying attention or not, your unconscious mind is always protecting you and working to keep you safe. One example of this is the unconscious mind (or autonomic nervous system) directing your immune system to protect you from infections and diseases like cancer. A second way is how it protects you by means of your automatic reflexes. For example, if you were to touch a very hot surface, before you even had time to think about it your unconscious mind would instinctively jerk your hand away. So, the unconscious mind has a protective function.

THE SUBCONSCIOUS MIND

This may surprise some people but the subconscious mind is who you really are. It is the source of all your habits, behaviors, beliefs, even your personality. Your subconscious mind really is an exceptional part of you, so let me teach you about it. Unlike the unconscious mind with its inborn instincts, reflexes, etc., the subconscious mind starts out completely empty. Then, as you go through life learning and having experiences you start to build up a database. The subconscious mind keeps a complete record or memory of our entire life going all the way back to the very beginning.

As those life experiences build they coalesce into beliefs and habits and once those things form, the mind tends to resist changing them.

The fact that our minds resist easily changing our beliefs and habits is both good and bad. It's good because it allows us to develop a consistent and efficient way of behaving in certain circumstances and around other people and this gives us a particular 'personality'. It's bad because when those habits and beliefs are holding us back, or are creating problems for us in some way, it is very difficult to make changes unless you have the ability and motivation to exert ongoing effort to make the change over time. Of course, the exception to this is hypnosis, because hypnosis can have immediate effect on the subconscious mind. We'll talk more about how this works later.

While it is the unconscious mind that generates our 'feelings', or the physical sensations that result from our emotions, the subconscious mind is responsible for generating our emotions. Based on our beliefs and experiences in the world, human beings respond to situations in an emotional way. For example, if you believe a person is treating you unfairly, the subconscious mind will begin to generate the emotion of anger. If it seems to your subconscious that your situation is unsafe or may become unsafe it will create fear. If you perceive the loss of someone or something important to you, the subconscious mind will cause sadness.

One of the most remarkable things about the subconscious mind is the fact that it seems to be unlimited in capacity. No one has ever filled it up. As long as your brain is healthy and working properly, you can always learn something new. The information in that database of the subconscious mind is a record of your entire life. Every life experience, everything we have seen, heard, felt, tasted, and smelled, whether we were consciously aware of it or not, all the way back to the beginning is stored in the subconscious mind and it becomes easily accessible in hypnosis. Even without hypnosis, people in their oldest years can tell you stories about their childhood. Even in situations where you don't remember something consciously, that information becomes very easy to recall in hypnosis. That's why hypnosis is sometimes used in court cases to uncover information about a crime.

Like the other components of the mind, the subconscious mind has a protective function. The subconscious mind protects against known dangers and generates emotions to motivate us to do the sometimes difficult things we need to do in order to fulfill our needs and desires.

THE CONSCIOUS MIND

Most people would guess that the part of their mind that makes them who they really are is their conscious mind. However, you've already learned what the truth is. The subconscious mind is who we really are. The part of our mind we like to think of as the 'thinking' part, or what we call our conscious mind, is really just our point of focus. Imagine your subconscious mind as a very vast, very dark warehouse of unlimited capacity. Now imagine you are wearing one of those miner's hats with the light on the front. Your conscious mind is like that headlamp and as you walk around inside the dark warehouse you can see wherever you choose to look and shine the light, whereas everywhere else is dark.

You could say the conscious mind has a home base in the present or whatever you're focusing on right now. For example, right now you are consciously focusing on reading these words but we could begin to talk about the past and the conscious mind could focus on the past, perhaps a pleasant memory. Then, we could start to talk about things in the future, like how your life might improve after the changes you want are made. You can begin thinking about the future and how hypnosis could give you a better life. It's useful to think about the conscious mind as primarily whatever you are focusing on right now, in the present moment.

The conscious mind is analytical and logical. It's a problem solving mechanism. It allows you to assess a situation, draw up experiences from the past, and use those experiences to formulate possible future scenarios. This allows you to plan and come up with the best possible solution. For example, if you're working on solving a math problem, you're using your conscious mind.

Another primary characteristic of the conscious mind is that it is very limited, unlike the subconscious mind which is seemingly unlimited. Remember the flashlight in the vast, dark warehouse. There is lots of scientific research that shows the conscious mind can only hold 5-9 bits of information at a time. This is why phone numbers are organized the way they are. This limitation is also one of the main reasons why attempts to make important changes in your life consciously (through 'willpower') generally fail. The very limited nature of our conscious mind, or focus of attention, means when our focus shifts to other things, our beliefs and behaviors return to subconscious control and go back on 'auto pilot' mode.

Hypnosis allows you to go in and work with the vast database of the subconscious mind, the part of your mind that makes you who you really are. In other words, hypnosis allows us to change our 'auto pilot' mode. Through Hypnosis you can have a tremendous effect on your habits, beliefs, and behaviors. Especially those limiting ones that have held you back and have prevented you from being as happy and successful as you can be.

As you saw from the chart, the conscious mind also has a protective function. It is constantly protecting you from what you perceive as dangerous based on what is rational and analytical.

THE CRITICAL FACTOR

You'll notice that between the conscious mind and the subconscious mind is something called the critical factor. The critical factor is a comparing mechanism. You can think of the critical factor as a kind of filter. As new information comes in through the senses, that information has to get through this critical factor before it can be accepted as true and have an impact on the habits, beliefs, and behaviors in the database of the subconscious mind.

This comparing mechanism or filter, the critical factor, is the biggest reason why it's so hard to change our habits, beliefs, and behaviors over time. When new information comes in, the critical factor compares it to what is already accepted as true in the subconscious mind.

If the new information matches what is already accepted as true by the subconscious, especially in regards to beliefs and habits, then it is instantly accepted. Once accepted by the critical factor, it goes in and reinforces those subconscious beliefs, habits, and behaviors to become more firm and exert a stronger influence in your life.

However, if the new information (true or otherwise) does not match what the subconscious mind has already accepted as true, it gets rejected by the critical factor and it goes into a different part of the database. It just becomes stuff you know about, but it's not accepted as true and has no effect on the beliefs, habits, and behaviors that govern your life. This process of accepting or rejecting new information based on what we already believe to be true is what scientists call 'confirmation bias'.

One of the primary reasons hypnosis is so powerful is because it bypasses the critical factor and allows us to make changes to the beliefs, habits, and behaviors in the subconscious mind and even in the unconscious mind. Now, it's time to learn more about what hypnosis is, and what it is not.

WHAT IS HYPNOSIS?

Many of us want to believe that magic is real. I get it. We want to believe that not everything has to conform to the sober, boring rules of the real world; and what could be more magical than hypnosis? I'm sorry to burst the bubble, but hypnosis is not magic. It is not a mysterious power exerted by a 'powerful' Hypnotist over a 'weak-minded' subject. It is part science and part art. Let's talk about what hypnosis **really** is.

From the previous section on how the mind works, it may already be clear to you that hypnosis is a natural function of the human mind. Hypnosis is quite literally an experience that people have all the time. We usually just don't call it hypnosis. We call it focus or being absorbed or concentration or even daydreaming. And even though hypnosis is named after the Greek word for sleep, it is in many ways the opposite of sleep.

Science has known for a long time that hypnosis is largely a state of laser-like focus. When a person is experiencing hypnosis, his or her attention is locked onto a single idea or thought to the exclusion of everything else.

Our modern understanding of hypnosis has evolved and developed over time. Going over some of the highlights of the history of hypnosis will help you understand our modern-day view of it.

A BRIEF HISTORY OF HYPNOSIS

Hypnosis is a function of the human mind. So it shouldn't be a big surprise the use of hypnosis, in its general sense, is found in cultures throughout history and across the world. Hypnosis has been around for as long as human beings have been around, likely back way before recorded history.

From as early as 3000 BC, hieroglyphics found on Egyptian tombs depict the use of hypnosis in religious ceremonies and surgical procedures.

The ancient Greeks also used hypnosis to prepare for surgery and other methods of healing. Natural human hypnotic states have been used all over the world and throughout history by native medicine men, tribal healers, Hindu Fakirs, shamans and others to heal both mind and body.

Franz Anton Mesmer (1734-1815) was probably the first to try to explain the phenomenon we now know as hypnosis as opposed to simply attributing it to some mystical power. Mesmer mistakenly believed that an invisible magnetic fluid flowed throughout nature and in every human body, that magnets could restore the balance of this magnetic fluid and thus cure the sick.

Mesmer used various methods, often using magnets, to induce a hypnotic trance. Mesmer became famous for his "Animal Magnetism" philosophy because despite the inaccuracy of his theories, his methods (which were hypnotic) were effective and resulted in many extraordinary cures. Eventually, the magnetic theory was debunked and Mesmer's trance-inducing methods became known as 'Mesmerism'. Obviously, this is where we got the term 'mesmerized'.

The name and much of our modern scientific understanding of hypnosis came from the pioneering work of the Scottish doctor, James Braid (1795-1860). After having watched a stage performance of Mesmerism, he became intrigued. But while Braid was fascinated by the idea of trance and it's possibilities, he rejected the notion that there was a supernatural explanation for it and set out to study it scientifically.

Based on Braid's early limited understanding, he coined the term "hypnosis" from the Greek 'hypnos' meaning sleep. Later, he realized that hypnosis is not a form of sleep but is actually a state of focused attention on a single idea. He tried to change the term from hypnosis to the more accurate term mono-ideism (one-thought) but the less accurate term 'hypnosis' had already stuck and its use remains today. He published his findings in Neurypnology (1843), arguably the first book on hypnosis.

Doctor John Elliotson (1791-1868), was a London physician who invented the stethoscope. He also performed over one thousand painless operations using hypnosis. Unfortunately, his success did not please his fellow doctors. The common medical belief of the day was that pain was necessary for healing. Despite Elliotson's low mortality rate and high success rate, his fellow doctors forced him out of medicine.

Another Scottish doctor, named James Esdaile (1808-1859) practiced as chief surgeon of a hospital in Calcutta, India. He used hypnosis in over 3000 surgeries and also found that hypnosis produced insensitivity to pain. At the time, the mortality rate during operations was normally up to 50%, but Esdaile found using hypnosis caused it to drop to just 5%.

French doctors Hippolyte Bernheim and Auguste A. Liebault formed the Nancy School of Hypnosis (1837-1919). Their efforts helped to demystify hypnosis and create an understanding of it as a normal human state. Their theory was that hypnosis was not caused by any mechanical means but by suggestion. Bernheim published his book 'De La

Suggestion' that proposed the power of suggestion as a powerful cure for both the mind and the body.

In 1895 Doctor Sigmund Freud co-authored his famous book "Studien uber Hysterie" with master hypnotist, Joseph Breuer. Unfortunately, Freud was not very good at inducing hypnosis. However, he found Breuer's work invaluable. In fact, it was largely due to Breuer's work with hypnosis that Freud was able to develop what he later became famous for psychoanalysis. Freud was so poor at hypnosis that eventually he abandoned using it altogether, choosing instead to simply use free association in a wide awake state.

It is ironic that despite the widespread notoriety of Freudian psychoanalysis, it is hypnotherapy that has proven to be far and away the more effective approach to making rapid and lasting change. One example of this is a comparison study published in American Health Magazine in 2007. The study showed that just 38% of participants undergoing psychoanalysis recovered after 600 sessions, while 93% of participants using hypnotherapy recovered after just 6 sessions. Maybe Freud should have worked a little harder at hypnosis.

During World War II (circa 1939-1945), hypnosis was used as a substitute for chemical anaesthesia in some prisoner-of-war hospitals. The medical staff found that hypnosis worked very well to eliminate pain as well as to speed healing. Because of its success, after the war doctors and other medical staff began spreading hypnosis to many fields of medicine including obstetrics, dentistry, dermatology and pain relief.

Other notable American hypnotists, including Dave Elman (1900-1967) and Ormond McGill (1913-2005), continued to increase public awareness and acceptance of hypnosis. Dave Elman was a noted radio host, comedian, and hypnotist. As a respected figure in the field of hypnosis and hypnotherapy, Elman taught hypnosis to hundreds of doctors across the United States. He also authored "Hypnotherapy", one of the most respected hypnosis books of all time.

American psychiatrist, Doctor Milton Erickson (1901-1980) is certainly one of the most well known contributors to the modern science of hypnosis and hypnotherapy. Erickson is best known for his use of a very naturalistic and indirect approach, both to induce hypnosis and to create positive therapeutic changes in his clients. While Erickson did not always use an indirect style, he did become the catalyst for an entire field of indirect hypnotic suggestion. Erickson was a master of metaphor and symbolic storytelling and his methods have been adapted by many leading figures in hypnosis today.

The work of Doctor Erickson was one of the primary sources of inspiration for the two gentleman credited for the creation of neuro-linguistic programming (NLP). John Grinder specialized in the study of language and Richard Bandler specialized in the study of subconscious processes. NLP is the source of a great deal of modern hypnotherapeutic technique. One of NLP's most famous techniques is known as the 'fast phobia cure' which reduced the time it took to effectively treat phobias from years down to, oftentimes, a single session.

Now that you've learned about some of the important history of hypnosis, let me fill you in on some of the latest advancements in the field. Recent research done on the brain, sleep, dreaming, and other fields of science have further clarified our understanding of what hypnosis is and how it works.

We now know that hypnosis activates the same process that the brain uses while dreaming, during what is known as the REM (Rapid Eye Movement) state. This process has been described as the brain's own 'reality generator' and it is why our dreams can be so realistic and believable to us while we are having them.

So, the truth is, going into a hypnotic trance is very common. Each night, without hesitation, we believe in the alternate realities our brain presents to us as we dream. For example, while bundled up for the night in our warm beds, fast asleep and dreaming, we can vividly experience ourselves in a blizzard, an icy wind blowing, knee deep in drifting snow. And not only do we believe we are there, but we can actually **feel** we are there. We can experience the wind blowing, the cold grip of freezing snow around our feet and legs, etc.

Even when not dreaming, many people are really quite good at imagining such a scene. Maybe you even found yourself vividly imagining the whiteness, intense cold, or the way an icy wind would feel on your face, as I was describing it.

Hypnosis activates this same natural 'reality generator' brain mechanism that all of us use on a regular basis, at least every night.

There is something else that is really important to understand about our brain's REM state. In humans, a fetus in the womb and the child early in life are pre-programmed in the REM state with the instinctive patterns (behaviors) that are needed for the different stages and circumstances of life.

Earlier, you learned about instincts during our discussion of the unconscious mind. But our brains don't just rely on pre-programmed instincts; we can learn new patterns. In fact, all new learning is the result of adding to or changing existing patterns in the brain and nervous system. And research is revealing that these new patterns are always learned in a REM (trance) state.

To summarize, hypnosis uses the same 'reality generator' brain mechanism we use when we are dreaming. This REM (trance) state allows our mental programming to be updated naturally as we grow in the womb and as we develop as children. As adults, it allows us to update our internal software through natural trance states as well as artificially with hypnosis.

It is important to remember that while hypnosis accesses the REM state, it is not sleep. Since hypnosis is a state of intense focus, in many ways it is actually the opposite of sleep. It is true that stage hypnotists and even hypnotherapists will sometimes use the word 'sleep'. If your hypnotist or hypnotherapist ever uses the word 'sleep' in the context of hypnosis, just think of it as a shorthand. 'Sleep' is shorthand for "close your eyes and go deeply relaxed, as if you were asleep." If someone were to really go to sleep they would miss the whole experience and their hypnotherapy session would become an expensive nap. Just remember, if your hypnotherapist says 'sleep', in the context of hypnosis, it simply means "eyes closed and deeply relaxed."

NATURALLY OCCURRING HYPNOSIS IS EVERYWHERE.

Hypnosis is a natural function of the human mind and people experience hypnotic states normally and frequently. One of my favorite examples of commonly occurring hypnosis is when a person is watching TV. I can remember watching my favorite tv program as a kid after getting home from school.

I could easily become so engrossed in it that my mom could stand right beside me and start talking to me and I wouldn't consciously hear a word she said because I was literally in a trance. I would remain 'entranced' and unaware (consciously) of my mom's presence until she broke my focus by standing directly in front of me. I would then finally realize that she was trying to talk to me. This is a prime example of a naturally occurring state of hypnosis.

Let me give you some more examples of common, naturally occurring states of hypnosis. Most of us can think of times while driving a car when we naturally began thinking about something else, like what we're going to do at work or on the weekend. Our focus shifts to something other than driving, our subconscious mind takes over the job of driving the car and we go into a naturally occurring state of hypnosis. Then, all of a sudden we reach our destination and we may wonder aloud; "Oh my gosh, where did the time go?" Or maybe we even missed our exit. This phenomenon is very common. We call it "highway hypnosis".

In one of the deepest levels of hypnosis people can experience what's called positive and negative hallucinations. Remember, a trance will activate the brain's 'reality generator' to one degree or another, like in a dream. A positive hallucination is when a person experiences something that really is not there. A negative hallucination is when a person does not perceive something that really is there.

This may sound bizarre but it's actually not that hard to fire up a sufficiently strong REM trance state to hallucinate. It happens to people frequently. Imagine a man making a sandwich for lunch. He looks over at the table and he notices there is no mustard on the table, so he says to himself, "Hmm, no mustard." He looks around the kitchen, and still seeing none, says to himself "nothing there."

He thinks it may be in the fridge. So, he opens up the refrigerator, and looking at the top shelf and seeing that there is no mustard there, repeats "not there". Moving down to the second shelf, sure enough, no mustard there, so he says to himself, "no mustard." And he continues to go down the shelves saying to himself, "nothing... nothing there... nothing there."

He really wants that mustard so his attention is focused as he turns to the shelves inside the fridge door. He may even use his finger to point to the shelves as he goes down each one saying, "no mustard, nothing, nothing." Perplexed, he then calls out to his wife, "Dear, where's the mustard?" She says, "It was in the fridge the last time I looked."

So, he refocuses his attention and begins looking at each shelf again going "Hmm, no mustard... nothing there... nothing there either." As he continues going through the shelves again, his wife walks up to the fridge, pulls out her magic finger, and just as it gets a few inches from that one shelf... poof! The mustard magically appears and the husband feels a little silly.

How in the world did that happen? How did he look right at that mustard bottle and not see it? It must have been right in front of him at least twice. He actually experienced natural hypnosis which, combined with an expectation of seeing no mustard, resulted in a negative hallucination. Meaning, he looked right at that mustard bottle (at least twice) and he didn't see it.

If you don't recognize it yet, here is how that happened: As the man focuses his attention intently on finding the mustard to make his sandwich, he begins to give himself variations of the suggestion "There's no mustard." By the way, people do this all the time too, it's called 'auto suggestion'. He then continues to go through the shelves of the fridge giving himself versions of the same auto suggestion, "no mustard, nothing there... nothing, nothing, nothing." By the time he actually lays eyes on the mustard his subconscious mind has accepted as "true" the idea that there is no mustard... nothing there. The information from the eyes gets reinterpreted by the subconscious mind and he hallucinates that the mustard is not there.

Now, for some people, it's a bottle of mustard. For the man's wife it may be her purse. For the next person it might be his car keys, or her glasses, that kind of thing.

One final interesting example is that in deeper levels of hypnosis people can also experience analgesia, which is a blocking of pain, or anesthesia, which is a blocking of all sensation. Nearly everyone has experienced getting undressed for bed and noticing a big bruise or maybe even a cut somewhere on their body. We wonder, "Holy cow, how did I get that?" During the day we can become so absorbed in an activity that as we focus, we often go into a natural state of hypnosis, then we incur the injury, the bruise, the scratch, or whatever, and we don't even feel it.

So, even seemingly bizarre and outrageous phenomena such as hallucinations, hypnotic analgesia and anesthesia, (and much more) are perfectly normal and natural for human beings, actually happen to people fairly frequently, and are quite easy to experience in hypnosis. These examples also help us to understand that we all go into a form of hypnosis naturally, practically on a daily basis.

You probably already understand this but it's worth repeating because it is important. Hypnosis is not only very natural but it is also safe. When you are formally hypnotized, you will always be conscious, just like in all the natural examples of hypnosis we've talked about. You're not unconscious when you are engrossed in a great movie, are you? Well, you'll also never be unconscious while doing formal hypnosis. When I ask a client to focus on something, that focus is a function of the conscious mind. No matter how deeply you go into hypnosis you will continue to hear the hypnotist's voice so you can continue to follow his or her instructions.

It is common for a hypnotherapist to have you focus on relaxation. Relaxation is a pleasant and often very useful thing to focus on. It's also common to become more relaxed as you progress through the hypnosis session. Because all the levels or components of the mind have a protective function, no matter how deeply you go into hypnosis you will always be safe and you will always be able to protect yourself.

Hypnosis is also safe in the sense that it is a natural process. Drugs can be helpful if used wisely. But it is indisputable that these powerful chemicals can also cause harmful side effects and, in many cases, can do more harm than good. This is especially true when they are used over extended periods of time. Surgery is also often dangerous and can cause negative consequences and side effects. Hypnosis, on the other hand, is a safe, natural, drug-free, surgery-free way to overcome challenges and make lasting positive changes.

Hypnosis is not only very safe but it is also very effective. Hypnosis was accepted by the American Medical Association in 1958. Hypnosis and Hypnotherapy, in various forms, have been used by medical and other professionals throughout recorded history. It is a proven tool used all over the world for a great variety of things from anesthesia to behavioral changes, psycho-somatic (mind-body) illnesses and many, many other things.

To illustrate this, let's revisit in more detail that 2007 study published in American Health Magazine I mentioned earlier. Researchers compiled metadata to compare the effectiveness among popular methods of therapy. Their results are below:

Psychoanalysis: 38% recovery after 600 sessions
Behavior Therapy: 72% recovery after 22 sessions
Hypnotherapy: 93% recovery after 6 sessions

Of course, these results reflect outcomes with well-trained professionals; inadequately trained practitioners won't get the same results. But, when it comes to the efficacy of hypnosis with a well-trained professional, this study is truly just the tip of the iceberg.

Hypnosis has been the subject of much scientific study. For those who are interested, a brief sampling of some of the more recent research for many of the most common uses of hypnotherapy has been included in Appendix I: Scientific Evidence for the Effectiveness of Hypnosis, at the end of this book.

You now know what hypnosis is and what it is not. We also went over some great examples of how hypnosis happens naturally all over the place. I have also talked about how hypnosis is safe and effective. That brings us to our next topic: What cool stuff can we do with this wonderful natural ability that we have other than ignore our mother while we watch tv, miss our exit, not see the mustard, or not feel that cut on our leg?

There are lots and lots (and lots) of beneficial things we can do with hypnosis. But, before we get into that, let me quickly point out that when we talk about hypnosis from now on, I'll be referring to formal hypnosis as opposed to all the naturally occurring stuff. Meaning, hypnosis between two or more people being used **on purpose**, for a particular reason or with a specific outcome in mind. The kind of hypnosis you would do with a hypnotist or hypnotherapist such as myself.

With that being said, one of my favorite official definitions of hypnosis is from the American Psychological Association. Which states:

"When using [formal] hypnosis, one person (the subject) is guided by another (the hypnotist) to respond to suggestions for changes in subjective experience, alterations in perception, sensation, emotion, thought, or behavior."

This definition builds on what we have already talked about

and is helpful in further understanding several key things about what can be achieved through hypnosis and hypnotherapy.

First, formal hypnosis generally requires a degree of cooperation; it is a collaboration. In other words, it's two (or more) people working together toward a common goal. This cooperative relationship is very much like a coach working with an athlete or a guide leading a client from one place to another.

A coach cannot force an athlete to improve. The athlete's success depends largely on his or her motivation to improve, willingness to follow the coach's instructions, and do the work.

Likewise, clients who have hired a guide to get them somewhere are not forced to follow. But, it would be pretty silly to pay good money to a guide and then not follow their guidance, right? The same holds true for hypnosis.

This is one of the reasons hypnotherapists commonly say that "all hypnosis is self-hypnosis." Clients must be willing and able to follow the hypnotherapist's instructions in order to get the positive results they want.

I would like to point out that people hypnotize themselves into doing things all the time. Remember, any time we are learning (changing patterns in the brain & nervous system) we are using, to one degree or another, a trance state.

Sadly, people too often use this amazing power in less than helpful ways. Frequently, people unwittingly use self-hypnosis to program themselves or others in ways that lead them to engage in all sorts of unproductive or downright harmful behaviors (i.e. smoking, eating too much, being terrified of tiny little insects, suffering unnecessary pain, etc., etc., etc.)

The good news is, with the help of a well-trained professional hypnotist or hypnotherapist, people can undo the negative or limiting programming that they have picked up and install updated empowering patterns that allow them to more easily overcome challenges and reach their goals. Below are some of the positive things that can be done with hypnosis based on the categories identified in the definition of hypnosis above:

- Alter subjective experience: Eliminating Fears, Phobias, etc.
- Alter perception: Perceive something that really isn't there (positive hallucinations) or not perceive something that really is there (negative hallucinations).
- Alter sensation: Cause a body part to feel warm or cold or light or heavy or numb (analgesia and anesthesia), or even increase sensitivity (sexual dysfunction or enhancement).
- Alter emotions: Resolve negative emotions like fear, anger, shame, sadness, etc. Increase positive emotions like joy, determination, love, forgiveness, and gratitude.

- Alter thoughts: Improve self image and self-esteem, be more mindful of past successes, reduce negativity and increase positive attitudes.
- Alter behaviors: Enjoy eating smaller portions, enjoy eating more vegetables and fruits, enjoy exercising, quit smoking, feel calm during stressful events, fall asleep faster, sleep more deeply, create the habit of a better golf swing, etc. etc. etc.

We'll talk more about these and even more wonderful things you can do with hypnosis in much greater detail in Part Two: Specific Applications of Hypnosis... so stay tuned.

WHAT TO EXPECT WHEN YOU GO TO THE HYPNOTHERAPIST

First, let me say every hypnotherapy practice is different. That being said, at **Boise Hypnosis** we offer potential clients a confidential and complimentary phone consultation. This gives potential clients the opportunity to ask us questions and to get to know us a little better. It also gives us a chance to talk with them about about the issue they want to work on, gauge their level of motivation, and determine if they are someone we want to work with.

If we choose to work with a new client, we usually take payment for their sessions over the phone. Clients pre-pay for their appointments because our appointments are given on a first-come, first-served basis and our schedule can fill up quickly. Pre-paying allows us to schedule all of a client's appointments at the earliest available times and close enough together to optimize their results.

At **Boise Hypnosis**, we pride ourselves on our ability to customize the hypnosis to each individual client. When new clients come into the office, they fill out some paperwork so that we understand relevant background, the problem, and the kind of solution the client expects. It's important to be thorough and the information clients give us always remains completely confidential and allows us to customize our approach to the client's unique situation.

Next, new clients usually watch a short video entitled "The Truth about Hypnosis" which complements the information in this book and prepares new clients to get the most from their sessions. After the video, clients have an opportunity to get answers to any remaining questions they may have and by this time new clients are usually eager to begin working on their goal with hypnosis.

At **Boise Hypnosis**, the actual process of hypnosis begins with an 'induction'. The induction process guides the client in creating a wonderful state of relaxation and focused attention. There are many ways to do this based on the client, his or her situation and personality.

The induction phase is generally followed by a process of deepening or intensifying the experience. You will find that the process of hypnosis is very pleasant and profoundly relaxing. You will find that you become more and more relaxed the further you go in the process.

Next, when the hypnotherapist observes that the client is ready he or she will begin the 'change work' for the session.

The hypnotherapist will guide the client through various exercises and/or provide various methods of suggestion and instruction to the subconscious mind leading it to create new patterns.

These new patterns, in turn, cause changes in how we understand things at a deep subconscious level and even at the unconscious level. Once these new patterns are accepted by the subconscious mind, they become the new default setting, so to speak. These changes to the subconscious and unconscious result in changes to how we feel, think, and even behave.

The last phase of the process is called the exduction. Here the client is gradually led to emerge from the profoundly relaxed state of hypnosis to a fully alert, more generally aware state, feeling refreshed and fantastic.

HOW TO MAXIMIZE YOUR RESULTS WITH HYPNOSIS

Let's talk about what **you** can do to ensure you get the best results possible from your hypnotherapy sessions. First of all, I want to reiterate that virtually every human being can be hypnotized and can benefit from hypnosis or hypnotherapy.

Remember, hypnosis is completely natural and is something virtually everyone experiences frequently. What that means is, if you are a human being of normal mental function - you **can** be hypnotised.

Many years ago, it used to be believed that only a certain percentage of people could be hypnotised. But now, we know that if you take the time to learn the truth about hypnosis, debunking the myths and misconceptions about it, and as long as you are willing to follow instructions, you can experience all the positive changes you want to make. By the way, leave it up to your hypnotherapist to determine if you are in hypnosis.

So, yes, you already have the natural ability to be able to do hypnosis. Like anything else, at first, some people will be better at it than others. In hypnotherapy, you will be using skills such as **concentration** and **imagination**. And while these things come more easily to some people than others, it is the nature of human beings to do better with practice.

My clients consistently report having a wonderful experience during their first hypnosis session. Then, they are pleasantly surprised to discover their second session is 10 times more powerful. That means that you will very likely find that regardless of your initial ability to do hypnosis, you will improve quickly. You may even surprise yourself with how rapidly you become an expert at going deeply into hypnosis.

To be successful with hypnosis, your willingness to **follow instructions** and to do the mind-work your hypnotherapist guides you to do is far more important than your initial ability or skill to do hypnosis. It is that inner drive to change that we'll talk about next.

A major key to your success with hypnosis is **your motivation to change**. In this regard, hypnotherapy is no different than any other form of therapy, or for that matter, any means of self improvement.

Whether you want to stop smoking, lose weight, write a book, be a better golfer, or a better parent, your motivation as a **participant** in the process is an essential ingredient to your success. If you make the mistake of thinking you can just take a nice nap while your hypnotherapist sprinkles magic fairy dust over you to make your problems go away, then you are fooling yourself and your lack of results will reflect it. As I mentioned earlier, hypnosis is not magic.

On the other hand, if you are truly ready for a change and you are willing to follow instructions, participate fully in the process, and do your part of the work, then good for you!

Because that means hypnosis will be a powerful force for positive change in your life! In my experience, good work can always be done no matter how challenging the issues, when the client is highly motivated. Therefore, I would suggest you dig deep and really think about those big reason **you** want to make this change. For those who could use a little help let's talk about how to connect to your most powerful motivations.

Whether your goal is to lose weight, become a non-smoker, overcome a phobia, make more money, or whatever, take some time to imagine the ultimate consequences of making **and** not making this change. People often find many of the most motivating feelings (positive and negative) involve the people they care most about. It's helpful to explore both the bad things you want to avoid as well as the good things you want to have by making this change. Many people find it helpful to write this down.

Here are the two big questions to really explore. They will help you dig deep and uncover your most powerful motivators to change:

- What are your greatest fears if you don't make this change?
- What potential positive benefits excite you most about making this change?

Carefully consider **both** these questions, one at a time, and become aware of what you would likely experience through all your senses. What I mean is, what specifically might you see, hear, taste, smell, and especially **feel** if these outcomes were your reality. What would you think of yourself? How would both outcomes impact the people you care about most?

Spend some time tapping into both your negative and positive emotions, be very specific, and come up with at least seven of your biggest fears, worries or concerns as well as seven of the positive benefits that would excite you most.

Also, notice which emotions (positive or negative) are the most motivating for you. Every person is different and there is no right or wrong answer to these questions. But, doing this exercise thoroughly should give you all the motivation you need.

It is also important to point out in this age of instant gratification, that another key to success I want you to keep in mind is that while hypnosis is a rapid therapy, it is wise to not expect persistent problems to disappear overnight. It is important to have realistic expectations. The famous author, Napoleon Hill wrote "Patience, persistence, and perspiration make an unbeatable combination for success". This wisdom holds very true for making all the changes you desire with hypnotherapy as well.

Remember the study quoted earlier, at 93% success after 6 sessions, hypnotherapy is much faster, much more affordable, and much more effective than other forms of therapy. Amazingly, while it may happen that an issue is resolved in just one session, most of my clients begin to notice significant changes after the very first session and the vast majority of issues are resolved in about 6 sessions.

Even in the extremely rare 'worst-case' scenario, if it were to take 10 or 12 or 15 sessions, a person will still get the best results, in the shortest amount of time, and with the least expense, with hypnosis. But again, most people only need about six sessions to make the change they want. It's worth taking the time and putting in the effort to have the lasting changes you want - to enjoy for the rest of your life, is it not?

Another important key to maximizing your results with hypnosis is to focus on one issue at a time. Occasionally, a client will come into my office with a whole laundry list of things she/he wants to change or improve. While it is absolutely true that hypnosis can address a wide array of different things, it is best to take one thing at a time. By focusing on one issue at a time you can bring all your mental and emotional resources to bear and get the best possible results in the shortest amount of time. In my experience, trying to do too many things at the same time leads to poorer results.

So, if you're like many people who would benefit from making several (or lots) of life-improving changes with hypnosis, simply write out a list of the changes you want to make and then prioritize them. You can put a number next to each one indicating the order of importance. Or you can rewrite your list, starting with the single most important issue at the top followed by the next important below it, etc.

One of the wonderful things about using hypnosis to make positive changes in your life is that oftentimes many of those issues further down the list will begin to disappear as you resolve the bigger, more pressing ones. That's the beauty of using hypnosis to make powerful and permanent changes to the patterns in your subconscious mind.

This concludes Part One: The Basics of Hypnosis. Next, in Part Two, you will have an opportunity to read through the specific applications of hypnosis you are interested in learning about. Learning about hypnosis is an important and wonderful thing; but, once you have the information you need, it is important that you **take action**.

Learning about hypnosis, in and of itself, won't get you those positive changes you want. So, be prepared to take the next step. Contact **Boise Hypnosis** and get started enjoying a better life!

CALL (208) 440-3306
For Your
FREE Phone Consultation!

PART TWO:
SPECIFIC APPLICATIONS FOR HYPNOSIS

Hypnosis and Hypnotherapy can affect powerful change in so many aspects of life, it would be virtually impossible to list them all. A partial list of some of the many ways to use hypnosis to improve our lives include: provide relief from chronic and acute pain; improve communication and enhance relationships; increase confidence, motivation, concentration, and memory; make achieving goals easier; manage stress and anxiety; overcome addictions, bad habits, eating disorders, insomnia, fears, phobias, procrastination, negative thoughts, problematic emotional and behavioral patterns: it is very effective at helping people to use their full potential at work, sports, writing, performance, art, public speaking, creative expression and much, much more. In this section we will go over, in detail, some of the most popular issues people come to see me for in my private hypnotherapy practice at **Boise Hypnosis.**

LOSE WEIGHT & KEEP IT OFF

Weight Loss is the most common reason people come to see me for hypnotherapy because weight loss is one of the areas I specialize. It is common knowledge that being overweight carries many serious health risks, can shorten your life, and can certainly impact your self-esteem.

So many people struggle to lose the weight and KEEP it off for good. Too often, a person will successfully lose weight, sometimes even a lot of weight, only to put that weight back on and then some. There are several reasons why this can happen. But, if you are ready to shed those pounds for life, nothing… and I mean **nothing** beats hypnosis.

Studies have confirmed that hypnosis with a well-trained hypnotherapist, skilled in weight loss, can be up to 30X more effective than 'willpower' alone. With the right hypno-therapist, hypnosis is the single most effective method to lose weight, and even more importantly, keep it off for good (see the studies referenced in Appendix I: Scientific Evidence For The Effectiveness of Hypnosis).

One of the biggest reasons certain kinds of hypnotherapy work so well for weight loss is because it deals with the cause(s) of the weight gain instead of just the symptom(s). In most cases, the primary causes of overeating are ultimately emotional. People eat to comfort themselves, or because they are bored, or due to stress, or maybe because it's time to celebrate. The list goes on and on. And often, people are not even consciously aware of the emotional reasons they eat. But whether the reasons are conscious or not, the one thing common to all these "reasons" for eating too much is that they are all emotions. The purpose of our emotions is to motivate us. And when our emotions drive us to overeat it's called 'emotional eating'.

What that means is, in order to lose weight and keep it off for good, the emotional cause(s) that are driving the urge to overeat must be identified and resolved. Experience shows these emotional drives are usually subconscious. Meaning, most people are often not even consciously aware of them.

They just know they can't seem to lose the weight and keep it off and they're not sure why. So, the fact that the likely cause of your extra pounds is in your subconscious is both good news and bad news.

The good news is, making changes to the subconscious is exactly where hypnotherapy excels. When we find and fix the emotional cause(s) that are subconsciously motivating you to do the things that make you fat, any diet will work far better for you. In fact, once you solve the emotional **cause(s)** of your overeating, the **symptom(s)** of being overweight will naturally begin to self-correct. Many people begin to lose pounds and return to a healthy weight without ever feeling like they are dieting.

The bad news is, until we find and fix the emotional cause(s), it is very likely that no diet will allow you to lose weight and keep it off for good. Even if you succeed in losing weight for a while you will likely gain it back and then some. Achieving and maintaining a healthy weight doesn't have to be frustrating. It's a problem that we solve very effectively with the kind of hypnotherapy we do at **Boise Hypnosis**.

Now is the time to take action. Shed the pounds and keep them off for good. Call us at **(208) 440-3306** and ask for a free phone consultation.

STOP SMOKING & OTHER ADDICTIONS

SPECIAL NOTE ABOUT ADDICTION: Addiction takes many forms. Virtually any substance or behavior can be used to excess. Even normally healthy behaviors like exercise can become harmful if taken to extremes. Some of the more common 'too much' behaviors that can become problematic for people include overeating, working too much, shopping too much, drug abuse, sex addiction, sugar addiction, gambling addiction, the list goes on and on. Addictive behaviors can and do destroy lives. Here we will focus on smoking but it is important to understand that all addictions operate on the same principles and all addictions can be effectively treated with hypnosis. There are two sections on addiction in Appendix I, one specific to Smoking Cessation and a second on Drug Addiction Treatment.

Certainly, one of the most well known applications of hypnosis is using it to stop smoking. The terribly negative consequences of tobacco to a person's health, relationships, finances, and even self image are also well known. The benefits of becoming a non-smoker for life are huge. As you will see in Appendix I, research shows hypnosis is almost certainly the single most effective approach to overcome the smoking habit for good.

People who feel ready to quit are offered many different methods to try to make it easier to stop smoking. Sadly, methods like drugs, nicotine patches, gum, and e-cigs almost always fail to help people permanently break the smoking habit because they only address the physical cravings for nicotine. Plus, most if not all of these methods can have negative side effects, are not natural or healthy, and may pose additional health risks.

The good news is that hypnosis has proven to be up to 15X more effective than willpower alone and is, by far, the most effective method for permanent smoking cessation. What's more, hypnosis is safe, natural, and very healthy. All of the 'side effects' of experiencing hypnosis with a well trained hypnotherapist are positive and beneficial. To review the evidence for yourself, see Appendix I: Scientific Evidence For The Effectiveness of Hypnosis, at the end of this book.

In addition to being healthy, safe, and natural, one of the biggest reasons hypnosis is far more effective for kicking the smoking habit for good is because it is holistic. Meaning, it can treat all the various parts of the habit, including the most important ones, the mental and emotional aspects.

For most smokers, the smoking habit is deeply rooted in the mind. Specifically, the subconscious mind. Most people who have smoked, started as children or teen-agers. When they decide to stop smoking it often proves to be very difficult. This difficulty demonstrates the power of the subconscious mind and the limitations of the conscious mind.

Despite being aware of the terrible costs and dangers of smoking and wanting to quit, people often find they continue to smoke anyway. As was discussed earlier in this book, the subconscious mind is far more powerful that the conscious mind and the subconscious simply overpowers attempts by the conscious mind to kick the habit.

Fortunately, as you learned in PART ONE of this book, hypnosis allows us to influence the subconscious in an effective and holistic way. Using hypnosis can reduce or even eliminate cravings and help holistically change a person's thoughts, feelings, and behaviors so he or she can become a non-smoker for life.

Now is the time to take action. Stop smoking for life. Call us at **(208) 440-3306** and ask for a free phone consultation.

END FEARS & PHOBIAS

We all experience fear from time to time. Fear is a perfectly natural response when we perceive something to be dangerous. A phobia is an irrational fear that can make it difficult for a person to function normally. A phobia is defined as an overwhelming and unreasonable fear of a thing or situation that poses very little real danger but still causes a strong anxiety response and avoidance. Most people with a phobia realize intellectually that their fear is unrealistic, but the fear causes a strong physical and psychological reaction that they can't seem to control.

Phobias often hold people back from feeling free to do the things they want and need to do in life. Phobias also frequently cause a secondary problem in that they often cause a person to withdraw out of fear that they will encounter a situation that causes their phobia. So, in other words, they develop a fear of experiencing the fear. This can severely limit their freedom. It can prevent them from doing things that they really want or need to do.

Any emotional experience perceived as dangerous can cause

enough trauma to trigger a phobic response. Phobias can even develop over time from a traumatic experience that a person has consciously long forgotten, because the subconscious mind remembers everything. A child can even learn a phobic response from a parent, relative, or other significant person in his or her life.

Symptoms of phobias can range from mild and annoying to severe and debilitating. The object or circumstances that the person is afraid of instantly and automatically triggers a fight-or-flight reaction in the brain. Sometimes, a person has a pretty good idea of the cause for their fear. But, often a person doesn't even know what caused the phobia in the first place.

Regardless of the circumstances, all phobias are formed in a similar way. One of the primary jobs of the the subconscious mind is to keep us safe. When a person finds themselves in a situation that the subconscious perceives as dangerous, it can link one or more things about the dangerous situation to an automatic fear response. Then, whenever the person's subconscious mind perceives circumstances as being similar to the traumatic experience, the subconscious mind will trigger the automatic fear response, a phobia.

Hypnosis and Neuro-Linguistic Programming are very effective at eliminating phobias. These tools are so successful because they reprogram the automatic subconscious reaction to the trigger, breaking the link, and installing a more appropriate response. This effectively frees the client from the fear once and for all.

Now is the time to take action. You can finally be free of the fear. Call us at **(208) 440-3306** and ask for a free phone consultation.

ENHANCE SKILLS & PERFORMANCE

Performance enhancement is a widely used application of hypnosis. Athletes, musicians, performers, sales people, business people, and more use hypnosis to accelerate development in their field and to outperform the competition.

Serious athletes and business people are often looking for ways to get an edge over their competition and take their performance to the next level. In sports, athletes know that physical conditioning will only take you so far. Hypnosis and related techniques have been valued to improve skills, overcome performance anxiety, optimize confidence, and rehearse ideal performance.

For decades, well-known athletes, actors, musicians, and other celebrities have worked with skilled hypnotherapists to achieve significant gains in their performance, regardless of their field. They do it because it works. They understand that whatever is going on inside your head has everything to do with how well you end up performing.

Previously in this book, we discussed that the subconscious mind is the driving force behind our motivation as well as the seat of our beliefs and behaviors. Hypnosis allows us to influence the subconscious in order to help an athlete or business person overcome issues of self-doubt which may be keeping him from moving to the next level. It can help a musician quickly learn a complex piece of music, or allow a dancer to fine-tune a technique. It can empower a level of self-belief and confidence which will enable you to excel beyond what you may have previously thought possible.

Hypnosis can also aid in acquiring the intense focus required to perform optimally. This relaxed state of intense focus is often referred to as "flow". Hypnosis can make all the difference in overcoming pre-game jitters, stage fright, the yips, or any other variation of performance anxiety, which can mean the difference between coming out on top versus being an "also ran". There are many great examples of great minds, famous stars and performers who have employed hypnosis to help them reach greatness. You'll find a big list of them in Appendix II at the end of this book.

One of the foremost examples is Eldrick Tont "Tiger" Woods. One of the most successful golfers of all time and one of the highest paid athletes in the world for several years, Tiger Woods is an excellent example of an incredible athlete who has used hypnosis to achieve a phenomenal level of success. He has reportedly been using powerful self-hypnosis techniques since his early teens. Self-hypnosis methods have helped him, like many successful athletes, quiet his mind, release anxiety, and become 100% focused as he plays the game. Such laser focus can be especially important in a game like golf where onlookers and other things can be very distracting. Tiger Woods has clearly shown how powerful hypnosis can be to conquer his mind and achieve extremely high levels of success.

Now is the time to take action. Improve your skills like never before. Call us at **(208) 440-3306** and ask for a free phone consultation.

IMPROVE ROMANCE & SEX

Hypnosis used within the context of sex, also known as erotic hypnosis, can really turbo charge many aspects of a couple's intimate relationship. We've already talked about many of the amazing things you can do with hypnosis. Most, if not all, of these unique abilities can be applied in sexual ways.

The first use is to eliminate distractions. We have already discussed at length how Hypnosis is all about focus. It makes sense that a couple more focused on each other will get more out of the experience. Hypnosis can allow distractions to fade away into the background or even disappear altogether.

Hypnosis allows you to be far more aware of your body, your own sensual feelings and your partner. Hypnosis can powerfully focus your attention on what matters most and away from everything else.

The next way you can utilize hypnosis to heat things up is to reduce or even remove inhibitions. Now, there is certainly a time and a place for inhibitions. Appropriate restraint does serve an important role in society. For example, you probably shouldn't go to work naked unless you live and work in a nudist colony. And punching people is generally a bad idea in the vast majority of contexts. That being said, there are times when inhibitions can prevent us from sharing fully and enjoying ourselves as much as we'd like.

A stage hypnosis show is a great example of how hypnosis can be used to lower a person's inhibitions and help them enjoy doing things they normally wouldn't do. Hypnosis can reduce or eliminate embarrassment or self-consciousness and allow a person who struggles with shyness to do the things he or she would really like to do but normally cannot. It can provide all the upsides to using alcohol to 'loosen up' with none of the downsides.

The third way erotic hypnosis can be used is to turbo charge our fantasies and role-play. Hypnosis is a powerful way to make a person's favorite fantasies far more vivid and realistic. Maybe your significant other has a favorite movie star you'd like to become or perhaps you'd like to make love in an exotic location or unusual situation.

For those of us who are fans of science fiction, hypnosis can be as if you have access to the holodeck on the starship Enterprise. Sexual situations that would normally be impossible, or very unlikely, can become your realistic experience. With hypnosis and perhaps a little practice tapping into the mind's 'reality generator', virtually any scene can actually FEEL real. With a little creativity, hypnosis can help you and your lover create sexual fantasies that are more realistic and exciting than ever. Hypnosis can help to give you both more of the good stuff you've always dreamed of having. Imagine the possibilities.

Earlier you learned that hypnosis is commonly used to reduce or eliminate pain. Well, hypnosis is very effective at modifying all kinds of sensory stimulation. Not only can hypnosis be used to decrease pain but sometimes it can be useful to decrease a partner's sexual oversensitivity as in cases of premature ejaculation.

By hypnotically reducing a man's responsiveness, his release can be delayed, increasing his staying power. For many men, this can help them feel much more confident about their sexual performance and their ability to please their partner.

In addition to decreasing sensitivity, hypnosis can also be used to increase sensual sensitivity and responsiveness. Sometimes it can be fun and very useful to make our most sensitive areas even more responsive. This can be especially useful for people who have less sensitivity than they would like either naturally or as a result of an an injury. With hypnosis you can even cause areas of the body that are not normally erotically sensitive to become so. Imagine turning an elbow or little finger into an erogenous zone. Think of the fun you could have with something like that.

Another favorite use of erotic hypnosis centers around the concept of control. This is a common theme in all kinds of sex play; dominant/submissive, master/slave, teacher/student, boss/secretary, etc. Many people get turned on by the idea of either taking control or giving up control in a sexual context.

Likewise, for many people it's a lot of fun to play with the fantasy of hypnotic control. While I have gone to great lengths to debunk the myths, hypnotising a partner or being hypnotised by a partner, combined with even just a light trance is often enough to be seriously arousing and can lead to lots of great orgasms. With a little more practice, imagine being able to cause a spontaneous orgasm in your lover with a snap of your fingers. How fun would that be?

Last, but not the least of the wonderful uses of erotic hypnosis is variety. Even the best relationships can become mundane at times. In my opinion, the more options and skills people have for exploring their sexuality the better. Combining hypnosis with sex can provide endless possibilities of fun and who wouldn't want that, right?

Now is the time to take action. Take your enjoyment to the next level. Call us at **(208) 440-3306** and ask for a free phone consultation.

DEFEAT ANXIETY & STRESS

Anxiety issues are all too common in the U.S. Sadly, this is one of the most common reasons people come to see me. Fortunately, it is also something you can successfully defeat with hypnosis, self-hypnosis, and other related tools that I teach.

Like many problems I help people deal with, there are varying degrees of anxiety. Nearly everyone has experienced some nervousness when it comes to things like public speaking, and hypnosis can certainly deal with them effectively. But generally when I talk about anxiety, I mean serious and debilitating anxiety disorders like full-blown panic attacks and Post Traumatic Stress Disorder (PTSD).

An anxiety disorder doesn't merely make a person uncomfortable or nervous, it impairs a person's ability to function.

Anxiety disorders, like phobias, often cause compounding feelings of anxiety or fear because they fear certain situations may be a trigger. This fear of triggering an episode can cause people to withdraw. It can prevent them from doing the things they want and need to do. It can cause them to miss out on opportunities, even negatively impact personal and work relationships.

Hypnotherapy has proven be an effective treatment in overcoming anxiety and the problems that come with it. Using hypnotherapy and related tools, we can identify the root cause of the problem and then work to fix it. I teach clients who come to me with anxiety issues powerful tools that they can use to quickly deal with anxiety at a moment's notice even when I'm not around. Having this easy and powerful tool at their disposal removes the secondary fear of experiencing a panic attack or other anxiety-related episode and gives them back a sense of control and tremendous peace of mind.

For less severe forms of anxiety, hypnotherapy is a recognised method for reducing feelings of anxiety. Hypnotherapy can be used to subconsciously reinforce a client's past successes, increase confidence and self-belief, while reducing feelings of fear, self-doubt, and worry. Hypnosis, together with the other powerful tools I teach, can help you develop and powerfully improve your ability to maintain a calm state of mind giving you much greater control over your feelings, as well as greater peace and tranquility.

Now is the time to take action. Free yourself from anxiety and stress problems. Call us at **(208) 440-3306** and ask for a free phone consultation.

REDUCE OR ELIMINATE PAIN

Chronic pain management may be the most extensively researched application of hypnosis. That's good because it's estimated that over 100 million Americans suffer from chronic pain in one form or another. Whether it's back pain, headaches, phantom limb pain, migraines, or any other form, pain is a terrible thing for a human being to have to endure day after day.

People trying to deal with chronic pain issues know all too well that the actual pain is just the beginning. Chronic pain, like many of the other problems we have talked about in this section, often is compounded by secondary issues like anxiety and depression and may prevent a person from doing the things they want and need to do to live a happy and fulfilling life.

When talking about pain, it's important to keep in mind that pain is nature's way of telling us that there is problem with the body. Of course, it is essential that you visit a qualified doctor to have the cause of your pain investigated. Frequently, pain is a symptom of a deeper problem and will disappear as the underlying problem heals. At other times, pain may simply be a temporary signal that you are overdoing it and you need to give your body a rest.

However, for our purposes here, we are talking about the kind of pain that, despite modern medicine's best efforts to resolve, becomes a chronic condition and continues to cause suffering day after day. In most cases, a person will be aware of the cause of the pain. The source may be an injury, joint pain, muscular pain, arthritis, back, neck, or shoulder pain, common headaches, migraines, phantom limb pain, or pain caused by a stroke or aggressive cancer treatment. In these kinds of situations, long-term pain no longer serves a useful purpose and becomes a source of misery, anxiety, and hardship for the person with the pain and their loved ones.

When faced with chronic pain, it's common for people to turn to drugs. Pharmaceutical companies have given us a wide array of chemical options to deal with pain, at least temporarily. Drugs such as Ibuprofen, Acetaminophen, Naproxen, Hydrocodone, etc. can help in the short term. However, prolonged use causes the body to develop a tolerance to the drug. Growing tolerance requires a person to take larger doses or switch medications entirely. Long-term use of painkillers becomes more and more problematic and can easily cause severe and potentially life-threatening issues including addiction, ulcers and other stomach problems, kidney and liver problems, increased sensitivity to pain, even depression.

Hypnosis is an all-natural, safe, and highly-effective solution to chronic pain that has been proven over decades. One of my earliest experiences with Hypnosis was seeing how effectively it can deal with chronic pain.

In the introduction of this book I talked about how as a teenager, the mother of one of my friends suffered almost daily with horribly painful and debilitating migraine headaches. She struggled with trying various drugs and injections but could never get the relief she needed. That all changed when one of her doctors suggested she use hypnosis. Hypnosis finally brought her the relief she needed. Seeing how Hypnosis helped my friend's mother was instrumental in setting me on the path to being a hypnotherapist.

Scientific research shows that hypnosis can alter how a person experiences pain and can have an effect on even severe pain. Amazingly, people all over the world routinely undergo dental and medical procedures like surgery in complete comfort while under Hypnosis without any other form of anaesthesia or analgesia (pain killing drugs).

In fact, in a recent review of controlled clinical studies, psychologists found that Hypnosis not only significantly reduced people's pain and their need for analgesics or sedation, but also reduced nausea and vomiting, as well as significantly reducing the length of stay in hospitals. It was also found that Hypnosis results in better overall outcomes and faster recovery times after a medical treatment (like surgery). You can learn more about many of the scientific studies that have been done on pain management by going to Appendix I in the back of this book.

Now is the time to take action. End the pain. Call us at **(208)** **440-3306** and ask for a free phone consultation.

FIND LOST ITEMS OR MONEY

I think everyone has had the experience of having misplaced something. You may think you remember where you last saw the item but then you just can't find it. Maybe you have even looked high and low for it. Often, the harder you look, the more frustrated you become, which actually makes it even harder to remember where you put.

We've all experienced this and it can be frustrating! People get busy and we all live in a world of stress, and with the hustle and bustle of life it can be very easy to misplace items or even money and terribly frustrating to find them. The good news, if if you have consciously forgotten, the memory of where your misplaced item is has almost certainly been stored in your subconscious mind. Hypnotherapy can help you to find your lost item by exploring the relevant memories in your subconscious mind.

Hypnosis is an ideal tool to access buried memories. One of the awesome things that happens when a person is in hypnosis is a phenomena known as hypermnesia which is a fancy word meaning a powerful enhancement of memory, or super memory, if you prefer.

As you have already learned, literally everything we experience, whether we are consciously aware of it or not, is stored in our subconscious mind. Using hypnosis we can quiet the conscious mind, work directly with the subconscious mind, and utilize the phenomenon of hypermnesia to go back in time to before the item or money was lost.

Once there the hypnotherapist helps you to meticulously retrace your steps, re-experience the moments prior, and re-create the details leading up to the loss or misplacement. Frequently, a client under hypnosis will come to a point in the process where he or she suddenly remembers the forgotten location and will suddenly exclaim "I know where I left it!"

Bear in mind, however, that a lost item is only recoverable when we have forgotten the true location. Obviously, it probably won't be possible to find your lost item or money if someone stole it, destroyed it, or moved it without your knowledge. There are times when items or money can fall out of our pocket, bag, or purse and we would not have been able to see it or be aware of it. In these kinds of situations, the problem isn't about a forgotten memory, so hypnosis won't be much help other than helping you deal with the sadness.

Now is the time to take action. Let us help you find what you've lost. Call us at **(208) 440-3306** and ask for a free phone consultation.

ENJOY EASIER SURGERY OR DENTAL WORK

Are you planning on having a surgery or have you recently suffered an injury? If so, hypnosis can help you heal more quickly, reduce the chance of complications, and help you get back on your feet in record time. Not only is hypnosis 100% natural, it is also very effective and has been used to help people undergoing surgery for literally thousands of years.

Amazingly, hypnosurgery goes back to, at least, the Egyptians. Hieroglyphics from 3000 BC depict hypnosis being used in ancient surgical procedures. In more modern times, doctors like John Elliotson (1791-1868) and James Esdaile (1808-1859) used hypnosis to perform literally thousands of pain-free operations. Additionally, while the mortality rate during operations had normally been 25-50%, using hypnosurgery it dropped down to 5%.

There are many ways hypnosis and related techniques can help make surgery or dental work easier. First, it can reduce nervousness and anxiety prior to surgery. Hypnosis can give a person the opportunity to rehearse a successful procedure preparing both the mind and the body for a favorable outcome. Hypnosis can also help promote wound healing and control blood flow, reducing the flow of blood during a procedure and increasing after the procedure to speed healing.

Next, hypnosis can reduce or eliminate pain from medical and dental procedures. Pain management is now becoming one of the best known medical uses of hypnosis. People all over the world routinely undergo dental and medical procedures in complete comfort while under Hypnosis without any other form of anaesthesia or analgesia (pain-killing drugs). If you haven't read it already, I've written an entire section on hypnosis to reduce or eliminate pain. Go check it out.

Post surgery, hypnosis can help a person to recover from anesthesia, and in addition to managing pain, it can minimize nausea and vomiting after surgery, and significantly reduce the length of time people need to stay in hospitals. Scientific studies have confirmed that Hypnosis results in better overall outcomes and faster recovery times after a medical treatment (like surgery). You can learn more about many of the scientific studies that have been done relating to this by going to Appendix I in the back of this book.

Now is the time to take action. We can help your surgery or dental work go much easier. Call us at **(208) 440-3306** and ask for a free phone consultation.

CALM IRRITABLE BOWEL SYNDROME (IBS)

IBS is a very common problem associated with the stomach and intestines. Medical professionals know that while IBS changes the way the gut normally functions, they won't be able to see any structural changes. IBS causes frequent abdominal pain and discomfort, as well as diarrhea, constipation or even a combination of both. These symptoms usually last for years after they start, but symptoms can stop and then start again. About 10-15% of adults in the U.S. suffer from IBS. It happens to be the most common problem GI doctors (gastroenterologists) deal with, and is among the top ten reasons people go to see a primary care physician. 70% of IBS sufferers are women.

A number of clinical studies have shown that hypnosis is a very effective treatment for irritable bowel syndrome (IBS). Qualified Hypnotherapists use progressive relaxation combined with suggestions of soothing imagery and sensations focused on the client's specific symptoms. People soon notice significantly less abdominal pain, constipation, diarrhea, and bloating, as well as improvements in overall well-being and quality of life.

Not only has research found that hypnotherapy can improve the primary problems associated to IBS, but it can also help relieve other IBS related symptoms like nausea, fatigue, backache, and urinary problems. Hypnotherapy is an effective holistic approach that improves not only the actual symptoms of IBS, but also treats the mental and physical components as well.

It's important to note that hypnosis can often enhance conventional approaches to treating IBS. But, hypnosis is not a license to ignore lifestyle factors like diet. Although, hypnosis can also help people who struggle with their diet to make better eating choices. For more information on the science supporting the efficacy of hypnosis for IBS see Appendix I in the back of this book.

Now is the time to take action. Calm your IBS. Call us at **(208) 440-3306** and ask for a free phone consultation.

Insomnia is a common problem. The National Sleep Foundation has found that 58 percent of people experience insomnia a few nights a week, or more. Insomnia can involve being unable to fall asleep, waking up in the middle of the night, or awakening too early in the morning.

Insomnia can sometimes be caused by other medical conditions, so it's a good idea to check with your doctor to rule out any underlying physical cause. Frequently, a person's insomnia is simply a result of stress: People lie awake at night worrying about problems or thinking of everything they should be doing during the day. Working with a Hypnotherapist and learning self-hypnosis can both eliminate the stress response as well as install better ways of dealing with stress.

In addition to the problems that directly result from a lack of proper sleep, not being able to sleep is frustrating. If insomnia continues to go unresolved, it can lead to other problems, including daytime tiredness, depression, irritability, impaired cognitive function, poor work performance, even accidents and injuries.

What's more, if you are experiencing prolonged periods of poor sleep or not enough sleep, you can be putting yourself and others at risk. For example, driver fatigue is one of the biggest contributing factors in car accidents.

Over time a lack of quality sleep can lead to chronic health conditions. A prolonged lack of sleep increases the risk of high blood pressure, stroke, heart disease, even cancer due to suppressed immune function. Poor sleep due to insomnia can make it difficult or impossible for your body and mind to renew and repair.

Recent studies have also found links between a lack of sleep and obesity. People who often don't sleep well are more likely to be overweight. There are several mechanisms whereby sleep influences both the body's metabolism and regions of the brain that control cravings for sweets and simple carbohydrates.

So, poor sleep interferes with proper metabolism and causes sleep deprived people to crave foods that encourage weight gain. Plus, it's very difficult to have the energy to exercise when you haven't slept well.

Sleep is also vital to our ability to learn and remember the things we learn. Adequate amounts of quality rest boosts memory, creativity, improves your problem-solving skills and allows you to balance your emotions. Insomnia can make daily activities more difficult, more dangerous, and will invariably impact your relationships and working life.

Hypnosis is an effective therapy for dealing with most forms of insomnia. Using hypnosis, a hypnotherapist can identify and resolve internal sources of stress and anxiety, help install more effective coping strategies to deal with stress in the future and can re-train the mind and body toward relaxation.

Hypnosis is a very relaxing and enjoyable experience and a useful tool for treating insomnia that is caused by stress. It's holistic, non-invasive, drug-free, and is relatively in-expensive.

I also teach clients to hypnotize themselves using self-hypnosis and often teach them other powerful tools to quickly and effectively deal with stress and anxiety at home or anywhere, whenever they have difficulty sleeping.

Now is the time to take action. Let us help you finally get the sleep you need. Call us at **(208) 440-3306** and ask for a free phone consultation.

PART THREE:
How to Hypnotize Yourself

First of all, let me start off by pointing out that there are many, many ways to do self-hypnosis. In fact, you may have already realized that we all hypnotize ourselves on a regular basis. Unfortunately, most people hypnotize themselves in negative, unhealthy, and problematic ways. Too often, we tell ourselves we are not good enough, too short, fat, ugly, etc.

The negative self talk we tell ourselves or receive from others can be a potent form of negative self hypnosis. Sadly, for many people the list of negative suggestions they habitually give themselves goes on and on. We fail because, in a very real sense, we hypnotize ourselves to fail. We focus on what we are afraid might happen (worry) instead of focusing on the outcome that we really want.

In this chapter I'm going to teach you one very simple and fun way to take control of your mind and to begin to program yourself for more success with self-hypnosis so your own powerful subconscious mind can begin to bring you more of what you really do want in your life and less of what you don't want.

Like anything worthwhile, self hypnosis takes some practice. However, it's our nature as human beings to do better with practice. You may be surprised at just how quickly you can get really good at doing self-hypnosis.

RELAXATION IS THE FIRST STEP

There are three simple, yet important parts to this effective self-hypnosis process. The first is deep relaxation. Deep physical relaxation encourages the "critical factor" of the mind to relax. Earlier in this book we discussed how the critical factor is the comparing mechanism or the "truth" filter of the mind that normally makes it difficult to change our beliefs and habits. Deep physical relaxation creates something called the "relaxation response" which is the opposite of the "fight or flight response".

An easy way to create this relaxation response for yourself is to, first, find a place where you can feel safe and comfortable. Turn off any electronics, put the pet in a different room and generally make this place as free from distractions as possible. Sit back in a comfy chair or recliner making yourself comfortable. If you're tired or think you may fall asleep it's probably best to sit upright.

Begin by closing your eyes and taking your attention to your eyelids. Did you know that you can relax your eyelids so much that they just won't work? You can. Try it. Relax your eyelids completely and then just hold on to that relaxation. As long as you maintain the relaxation in your eyelids, they won't work. It's basic physiology. Any muscle (including your eyelid muscles) can not be relaxed and flexed at the same time. If your eyes open you will immediately know that you removed the relaxation. Keep working at it until you can relax your eyelids and maintain the relaxation. You'll know when you are doing it correctly because even when your eyebrows move, your eyelids will remain closed when you test them. When you can do this congratulate yourself. Well done. You are ready for the next step.

Once you have created enough relaxation in your eyelids that they won't work, allow that relaxation to begin to spread up into the top of your head. Relax the top of your head just like your eyelids are relaxed. Now, send that relaxation all the way down your body like a wonderful wave of relaxation.

Allow that wave of relaxation to relax every muscle of your body as it flows down your body. Feel your muscles letting go and releasing all the way down to the bottoms of your feet.

Next, you simply return your attention to your eyelids and repeat the process. Relaxing your eyelids even more. Perhaps you'll choose to relax your eyelids 10 times more than before or maybe you'll just want to double the relaxation. Whatever you decide when you are confident you have created that level of relaxation in your eyelids you can give them a check and notice again how they stay closed.

Then allow the deeper relaxation to spread up into the top of your head, relaxing the top of your head even more, just like your eyelids are relaxed. Then send that deeper relaxation down your entire body like a wave of relaxation. Feel the muscles letting go even more as that wave of relaxation flows down your entire body all the way down to the bottoms of your feet.

Continue this process at least three times. You can do it more if you like. You'll find that the deeper relaxed you go, the better you will feel. Just remember, you don't want to go too deep or it will be difficult to follow the next steps you are about to learn. Again, the relaxation response that you are creating allows the critical factor to relax so that you can make changes to the subconscious (& unconscious) mind using the next two key components.

USE THE POWER OF YOUR IMAGINATION

The second key element to self-hypnosis is imagination. Your imagination has a powerful effect on your subconscious mind. Simply use your imagination to create a representation of what you want. It's important to imagine what we DO want and not what we DO NOT want, as the subconscious mind will act to create more of what we focus on.

This representation of what you want can be visual, it can be based on what you might hear, it can be based on what you might physically feel. In fact, by far the very best way is to incorporate all of the senses into our imagining. Allow yourself to experience what you want as if your mind were like the holodeck of Star Trek fame. Imagine the scene in 3D, full color. Imagine hearing the sounds clearly. Feel the clothes you are wearing, the temperature of the air, feel your body moving as you perform the actions.

Make your imagined experience as vivid, clear, and detailed as you can. Remember to keep it positive. Once you have done that you are ready to add the third, and arguably most important, element to your self-hypnosis practice.

Now that you are deeply relaxed and imagining the outcome that you want as vividly as you can, you are ready to add in the third vital part of the process, emotion. Ask yourself, How would you feel if your imagined experience were reality? What positive emotions would you want to experience if what you are imagining were true? Would you feel joy? How about pride or a sense of accomplishment? Allow those emotions to come up, feel them growing stronger and stronger in your body. You can even stack these positive emotional states one on top of another causing them to blend and build.

This process is very powerful; but I have a tip that will turbo-charge it, making the whole thing 10 times more powerful for you. Are you ready to hear it? Here it is. Once you have added in all the emotional states you want, begin to allow yourself to feel a sense of GRATITUDE as if you already had what you want. The feeling of gratitude is so powerful because it clearly communicates what you want to the subconscious mind. Gratitude is the ultimate emotion of receivership. It gives your subconscious mind the experience of having what you want. And as you continue to practice, your subconscious will begin to create more and more of it in your reality.

The fastest and easiest way to learn self-hypnosis is by working directly with a professional hypnotherapist. If you would like to know more about learning self-hypnosis call us at **(208) 440-3306.**

APPENDIX I:
SCIENTIFIC EVIDENCE FOR
THE EFFECTIVENESS OF HYPNOSIS

I consider myself a skeptic. You may be skeptical too, and that's perfectly okay. I admire a person who can question things and think for themselves. So, what real evidence is there that hypnosis is effective? While science doesn't understand everything about the brain, the mind, or hypnosis yet, there has been lots of research on hypnosis.

The first thing I want to point out is that one of the things we do know about hypnosis is that it has an impact on the brain that can be measured scientifically with instruments. David Spiegel, from Stanford University, is one of America's leading psychiatrists. David and his team scanned the brains of volunteers who were told, while under hypnosis, that they were looking at objects in full-color. However, in reality the objects were in black and white.

Brain scans showing areas of the brain that register color had significantly increased blood flow, meaning that the hypnotised volunteers were genuinely 'seeing' colors, as they had been instructed. This is strong scientific evidence that something happens in the brain when people are hypnotised that doesn't happen when they are not experiencing a hypnotic state.

Professional hypnotists and hypnotherapists, like myself, have been successfully using hypnotic techniques and have known all along that hypnosis has a real and powerful effect on how both the mind and body function.

Hypnosis, or more precisely hypnotherapy, is one of the most studied methods of behavioural change. Here is some of the researched evidence:

WEIGHT LOSS

Hypnosis is Over 30 Times as Effective for Weight Loss
The effects of hypnosis on weight loss was investigated for 60 females who were at least 20% overweight. Treatment included hypnosis for ego-strengthening, decision making and motivation, ideomotor exploration in individual hypnosis, and group hypnosis with maintenance suggestions. Hypnosis was far more effective than a control group. At follow-up, the hypnosis group lost an average of 17 lbs while the control group lost an average of 0.5 lbs.

Source: Cochrane, Gordon; Friesen, J. (1986). Hypnotherapy in weight loss treatment. Journal of Consulting and Clinical Psychology, 54, 489-492.

Hypnosis More Than Doubled Average Weight Loss
Study of the effect of adding hypnosis to cognitive-behavioral treatments for weight reduction. Additional data was obtained from authors of two studies. Analyses indicated that the benefits of hypnosis increased substantially over time.

Source: Kirsch, Irving (1996). Jou. of Consulting and Clinical Psych., 64 (3), 517-519.

Hypnosis Showed Significantly Lower Post-Treatment Weights

Two studies compared overweight smoking and non-smoking adult women in a hypnosis-based, weight-loss program. Both achieved significant weight losses and decreases in Body Mass Index. Follow-up study replicated significant weight loss and declines in Body Mass Index. The hypnosis program yielded significantly lower post-treatment weights and a greater average number of pounds lost.

Source: Johnson DL, Psychology Reprints. 1997 Jun; 80 (3 Pt 1):931-3.

Hypnotherapy group with stress reduction achieved significantly more weight loss than the other two treatments

Randomized, controlled, parallel study of two forms of hypnotherapy (directed at stress reduction or energy intake reduction), vs dietary advice alone in 60 obese patients with obstructive sleep apnoea on nasal continuous positive airway pressure treatment.

Source: J. Stradling, D. Roberts, A. Wilson and F. Lovelock, Churchill Hospital, Oxford, OX3 7LJ, UK

Hypnosis can more than double the effects of traditional weight loss approaches

An analysis of five weight loss studies reported in the Journal of Consulting and Clinical Psychology in 1996 showed that the "weight loss reported in the five studies indicates that hypnosis can more than double the effects" of traditional weight loss approaches.

Source: University of Connecticut, Journal of Consulting and Clinical Psychology in 1996 (Vol. 64, No. 3, pgs 517-519).

Weight loss is greater where hypnosis is utilized
Research into cognitive-behavioral weight loss treatments established that weight loss is greater where hypnosis is utilized. It was also established that the benefits of hypnosis increase over time.

Source: Journal of Consulting and Clinical Psychology (1996)

Hypnosis: Effective Way To Lose Weight
A study of 60 females who were at least 20% overweight and not involved in other treatment showed hypnosis is an effective way to lose weight.

Source: Journal of Consulting and Clinical Psychology (1986)

SMOKING CESSATION

Hypnosis Most Effective Says Largest Study Ever: 3 Times as Effective as Patch and 15 Times as Effective as Willpower
Hypnosis is the most effective way of giving up smoking, according to the largest ever scientific comparison of ways of breaking the habit. A meta-analysis, statistically combining results of more than 600 studies of 72,000 people from America and Europe to compare various methods of quitting. On average, hypnosis was over three times as effective as nicotine replacement methods and 15 times as effective as trying to quit alone.

Source: University of Iowa, Journal of Applied Psychology, How One in Five Give Up Smoking. October 1992. (Also New Scientist, October 10, 1992.)

90.6% Success Rate for Smoking Cessation Using Hypnosis
The University of Washington School of Medicine reported that 39 out of 43 patients undergoing hypnosis to stop smoking cessation remained non-smokers at follow-up. (6 months to 3 years post-treatment). This represents a 90.6% success rate using hypnosis.

Source: Int J Clin Exp Hypn. 2001 Jul;49(3):257-66. Barber J.

87% Reported Abstinence From Tobacco Use With Hypnosis
A study of 93 male and 93 female outpatients used hypnosis to stop smoking. At 3-month follow-up, 86% of the men and 87% of the women reported to be tobacco-free.

Source: Johnson DL, Karkut RT. Adkar Associates, Inc., Bloomington, Indiana. Psychol Rep. 1994 Oct; 75(2):851-7. PMID: 7862796 [PubMed - indexed for MEDLINE]

81% Reported They Had Stopped Smoking After Hypnosis
At Texas A&M University twenty-one smokers, referred by their primary physician, had an initial consultation and then had three hypnosis sessions for smoking cessation. At the end of treatment, 81% of those patients reported that they had stopped smoking, and 48% reported abstinence at 12 months post-treatment.

Source: Int J Clin Exp Hypn. 2004 Jan; 52(1):73-81. Elkins GR, Rajab MH.

Hypnosis Patients Twice As Likely To Remain Smoke-Free After Two Years

Study of 71 smokers showed that after a two-year follow up, patients that quit with hypnosis were twice as likely to remain smoke-free than those who quit on their own.

Source: Wynd, CA. Journal of Nursing Scholarship, 2005; 37:3, pages 245-250.

Hypnosis More Effective Than Drug Interventions For Smoking Cessation

Group hypnosis sessions, evaluated at a less effective success rate (22% success) than individualized hypnosis sessions. However, group hypnosis sessions were still demonstrated here as being more effective than drug interventions.

Source: Ohio State University, College of Nursing, Columbus, OH 43210, USA Descriptive outcomes of the American Lung Association of Ohio hypnotherapy smoking cessation program. Ahijevych K, Yerardi R, Nedilsky N.

PAIN MANAGEMENT

Hypnosis Reduces Frequency and Intensity of Migraines

Study compared the treatment of migraine by hypnosis and autohypnosis with the treatment of migraine by the drug prochlorperazine (Stemetil). Results show that the number of attacks and the number of people who suffered blinding attacks were significantly lower for the group receiving hypnotherapy than for the group receiving prochlorperazine. For the group on hypnotherapy, these two measures were significantly lower when on hypnotherapy than when on the previous treatment. It is concluded that further trials of hypnotherapy are justified against some other treatment not solely associated with the ingestion of tablets.

Source: Anderson JA, Basker MA, Dalton R, Migraine and hypnotherapy, International Journal of Clinical & Experimental Hypnosis 1975; 23(1): 48-58.

Hypnosis Has a Reliable and Significant Impact on Acute and Chronic Pain

Hypnosis has been demonstrated to reduce pain. Studies on the mechanisms of laboratory pain reduction have provided useful applications to clinical populations. Studies showing central nervous system activity during hypnotic procedures offer preliminary information concerning possible physiological mechanisms of hypnotic analgesia. Randomized controlled studies with clinical populations indicate that hypnosis has a reliable and significant impact on acute and chronic pain conditions.

Source: Hypnosis and clinical pain. Patterson DR, Jensen MP, Department of Rehabilitation Medicine, University of Washington School of Medicine, Seattle, WA USA 98104 Psychol Bull. 2003 Jul; 129(4):495-521.

Hypnosis Reduces Pain Intensity

Analysis holding both groups and conditions constant,

revealed that application of hypnotic analgesia reduced report of pain intensity significantly more than report of pain unpleasantness.

Source: Dahlgren LA, Kurtz RM, Strube MJ, Malone MD, Differential effects of hypnotic suggestion on multiple dimensions of pain. Journal of Pain & Symptom Management. 1995; 10(6): 464-70.

Hypnosis Lowered Post-treatment Pain in Burn Injuries
Patients in the hypnosis group reported less post treatment pain than did patients in the control group. The findings are used to replicate earlier studies of burn pain hypnoanalgesia.

Source: Patterson DR, Ptacek JT, Baseline pain as a moderator of hypnotic analgesia for burn injury treatment. Journal of Consulting & Clinical Psych. 1997; 65(1): 60-7.

Hypnosis Lowered Phantom Limb Pain
Hypnotic procedures appear to be a useful adjunct to established strategies for the treatment of phantom limb pain and would repay further, more systematic, investigation.

Source: Treatment of phantom limb pain using hypnotic imagery. Oakley DA, Whitman LG, Halligan PW, Department of Psychology, University College, London, UK.

Fibromyalgia: Hypnosis is a Powerful Tool in Pain Therapy
Attempting to better understand mechanisms behind hypnotic analgesia, we measured regional brain blood flow

with positron emission tomography in patients with fibromyalgia, during both hypnotically-induced analgesia and resting wakefulness. Patients experienced less pain during hypnosis than at rest. The observed blood-flow pattern supports notions of a multifactorial nature of hypnotic analgesia.

Source: Functional anatomy of hypnotic analgesia: a PET study of patients with fibromyalgia. Wik G, Fischer H, Bragee B, Finer B, Fredrikson M, Department of Clinical Neurosciences, Karolinska Institute and Hospital, Stockholm, Sweden Eur J Pain. 1999 Mar; 3(1):7-12.

Hypnosis Reduces Pain of Headaches and Anxiety
The improvement was confirmed by the subjective evaluation data gathered with the use of a questionnaire and by a significant reduction in anxiety scores.

Source: Melis PM, Rooimans W, Spierings EL, Hoogduin CA, Treatment of chronic tension-type headache with hypnotherapy: a single-blind time controlled study. Headache 1991; 31(10): 686-9.

DRUG ADDICTION TREATMENT

Significantly More Methadone Addicts Quit with Hypnosis. 94% Remained Narcotic Free
Significant differences were found on all measures. The experimental group had significantly less discomfort and illicit drug use, and a significantly greater amount of cessation. At six month follow up, 94% of the subjects in the

experimental group who had achieved cessation remained narcotic free.

Source: Comparative study of hypnotherapy & psychotherapy in the treatment of methadone addicts. American Journal of Clinical Hypnosis, 1984; 26(4): 273-9.

Hypnosis Shows 77 Percent Success Rate for Drug Addiction

Treatment has been used with 18 clients over the last 7 years and has shown a 77 percent success rate for at least a 1-year follow-up. 15 were being seen for alcoholism or alcohol abuse, 2 clients were being seen for cocaine addiction, and 1 client had a marijuana addiction.

Source: Intensive Therapy- Utilizing Hypnosis in the Treatment of Substance Abuse Disorders. Potter, Greg, American Journal of Clinical Hypnosis, Jul 2004.

Self-Hypnosis Raises Self-esteem and Serenity. Lowered Impulsivity and Anger

In a research study on self-hypnosis for relapse prevention with chronic drug/alcohol users. 261 participants admitted to Substance Abuse Residential Rehabilitation Treatment Programs. Individuals who used self-hypnosis "at least 3 to 5 times a week," at 7-week follow-up, reported the highest levels of self-esteem and serenity, and the least anger/impulsivity, in comparison to the minimal-practice and control groups.

Source: American Journal of Clinical Hypnotherapy 2004 Apr; 46(4):281-97)

Dual Study: Healed 41% faster from fracture: Healed significantly faster from surgery
Two studies from Harvard Medical School show hypnosis significantly reduces the time it takes to heal. Study One: Six weeks after an ankle fracture, those in the hypnosis group showed the equivalent of eight and a half weeks of healing. Study Two: Three groups of people studied after breast reduction surgery. Hypnosis group healed "significantly faster" than supportive attention group and control group.

Source: Harvard University Gazette Online at http://www.hno.harvard.edu/gazette/2003/05.08/01-hypnosis.html.

Hypnosis Reduces Pain and Speeds Recovery from Surgery
Since 1992, we have used hypnosis routinely in more than 1400 patients undergoing surgery. We found that hypnosis used with patients as an adjunct to conscious sedation and local anesthesia was associated with improved intraoperative patient comfort, and with reduced anxiety, pain, intraoperative requirements for anxiolytic and analgesic drugs, optimal surgical conditions and a faster recovery of the patient. We reported our clinical experience and our fundamental research.

Source: [Hypnosis and its application in surgery] Faymonville ME, Defechereux T, Joris J, Adant JP, Hamoir E, Meurisse M, Service d'Anesthesie-Reanimation, Universite de Liege, Rev Med Liege. 1998 Jul; 53(7):414-8.

Hypnosis Useful in Hospital Emergency Rooms

Hypnosis can be a useful adjunct in the emergency department setting. Its efficacy in various clinical applications has been replicated in controlled studies. Application to burns, pain, pediatric procedures, surgery, psychiatric presentations (e.g., coma, somatoform disorder, anxiety, and post traumatic stress), and obstetric situations (e.g., hyperemesis, labor, and delivery) are described.

Source: Emerg Med Clin North Am. 2000 May; 18(2):327-38, x. The use of hypnosis in emergency medicine. Peebles-Kleiger MJ, Menninger School of Psychiatry and Mental Health Sciences, Menninger Clinic, Topeka, KS, USA. peeblemj@menninger.edu

APPENDIX II:
FAMOUS PEOPLE WHO HAVE USED HYPNOSIS

This list is certainly not complete and does not include the countless Pro & Olympic athletes who use 'guided imagery' and related methods which are also hypnosis. This list only includes many famous people who have used 'formal hypnosis' as defined in this book.

Royalty
Sarah Ferguson, Duchess of York (Weight Loss & Nail Biting)
Duchess Kate Middleton (Hypno-Birthing & Morning Sickness)
Princess Diana (Public Speaking & Confidence)

Actors
Kevin Costner (Sea Sickness)
Matt Damon & Ellen DeGeneres (Smoking)
Drew Barrymore (Smoking)
Orlando Bloom (Chocolate Addiction)
Ashton Kutcher, Charlize Theron, & Ben Affleck (Smoking)
Emily Deschanel & Jessica Alba (Hypno-Birthing)
Sylvester Stallone (Filming "Rocky"-1975)
Bruce Willis & James Earl Jones (Stuttering)
Katy Perry & Winona Ryder (Smoking)
Samuel Jackson & Debra Messing (Smoking)

Singers
Billy Joel, Brittney Spears (Smoking)
Fergie, lead singer for Black-Eyed Peas (Weight Loss)
Tony Curtis (Fear of Flying)

Professional Athletes
Tiger Woods & Jack Nicklaus (Golf Performance)

Miscellaneous
Martha Stewart (Nightmares) Simon Cowell (Smoking)

Justin Timberlake, Sean Penn, Dolly Parton, Lily Tomlin & Mel Gibson have all used hypnosis to overcome various challenges and improve their lives. Again, this is by no means a comprehensive list. You can easily confirm the information above and learn more about their individual stories by searching the internet.

SEIZE THE MOMENT!

I sincerely hope you have found this book helpful and that it has given you the information and encouragement you need to use hypnosis to unleash the tremendous power of your own mind. As a human being, you are endowed with a super powerful subconscious mind. A subconscious mind that can help you make all the positive changes you desire - through hypnosis.

I hope you have been inspired to seize this moment. Now is the time to take action toward making the changes in your life that will allow you to use hypnosis to leave your challenges behind and to embrace those new ways of thinking and acting that begin to bring you the success, peace and happiness that you desire.

Boise Hypnosis is here to help you make the positive changes you want a reality in your life. Go to our offical website at www.BoiseHypnotherapist.com or call (208) 440-3306 to discuss your issue(s) with a well-trained professional hypnotherapist and discover if we are a good fit for each other. We have a wide selection of hypnotherapy packages designed to optimize your results. **Do it today**. You will be glad you did.

Don't Just Take My Word For It: A Few Testimonials
Katherine R. in Boise wrote on Yelp: "I can't RAVE enough about this fabulous, master hypnotist.

I have been a fan of hypnosis for many years; it has helped me stop smoking among other things and I have been to many hypnotists over the years. I have read books and used tapes and been to clinics.

Since hypnosis certificates are pretty easy to get, you get a lot of people in this field who just are not that good or experienced, not to mention some horrible rip-off companies who charge thousands of dollars for a contract.

There is no reason to buy a contract from a chain like Positive Changes when, in fact, if you see a great hypnotist like John who has made hypnosis his life's work, one-on-one, you will get much better results...

John is gifted and has in-depth knowledge that is rare and which you will never get from employees hired by a chain. John is one of the best hypnotists I have ever experienced, he also puts you right at your ease and his prices are very reasonable.

I plan to work with him on several issues, one at a time. I saw results in my first session which is something you rarely find. He's great!"

Harold H. in Boise wrote on Yelp: "Boise Hypnosis is a wonderful place to get hypnotherapy done. John Wylie is an expert and he makes sure that you are feeling better after your session. If you need a reliable hypnotherapist to resolve your habits, vices, worries, or to stop smoking, give him a call!"

Astrid M. in Boise wrote on Google: "I'm very happy that I found John. I've been fighting depression for over a year and have gained over 50lbs and taking prescription medicine.

With the therapy and tools he has given me I feel much better. After the 3rd session I was already seeing results. I'm now losing weight and not needing my medicine. I highly recommend him!!!"

Katrina C. in Boise wrote on Google: "John is an amazing hypnotist. He is very good at what he does... If you are looking for an awesome and amazing hypnotist, then look no further. John Wylie is your hypnotist."

Mary L. in Boise wrote on Google: "I would definitely recommend Boise Hypnosis to everyone who feels like they have something to work on to better themselves, etc. I had the best experience and great results!"

Lisa M. in Boise wrote: "I have been seeing great improvements since I began my sessions. After just one appointment I noticed a real difference. I'm excited to see continued improvement with additional sessions."

Gary S. in Boise wrote: "What I really liked about working with Boise Hypnosis, besides the great results I got, was the trust and good feeling I received working with John. He made me feel safe and he was very professional. He's a top notch hypnotist who I will certainly refer others to."

Dorene F. in Boise wrote: "After seeing John Wylie at Boise Hypnosis I have been doing so well. I have lost weight, I feel so much more relaxed and free of stress. I've been worrying less and i'm sleeping better than I have in a long while. John has given me the confidence to do what I need to do. Thank you!"

www.ingramcontent.com/pod-product-compliance
Lightning Source LLC
Chambersburg PA
CBHW050418290526
45786CB00003B/1315